Dress Up
Your Dog

Dress Up Your Dog

ANNETTE HOWARD

THUNDER BAY
P·R·E·S·S

San Diego, California

THUNDER BAY
P · R · E · S · S

Thunder Bay Press
An imprint of the Advantage Publishers Group
10350 Barnes Canyon Road, San Diego, CA 92121
www.thunderbaybooks.com

All notations of errors or omissions should be addressed to Thunder Bay Press,
Editorial Department, at the above address. All other correspondence (author
inquiries, permissions) concerning the content of this book should be addressed to
BlueRed Press Ltd, 6 South Street, Totnes, Devon, TQ9 5DZ, UK,
or e-mail: info@blueredpress.com

ISBN 13: 978-1-59223-876-7
ISBN 10: 1-59223-876-9

Printed in China

1 2 3 4 5 12 11 10 09 08

CONTENTS

INTRODUCTION

Some people might think that dressing up a dog in silly outfits is unnecessary, or even a little cruel. After all, you wouldn't expect to see a wolf dressed up outside a fairy tale, so why inflict it on the wolf's descendant? If you're a dog owner, though, it will probably have crossed your mind from time to time how human your companion can be; the longer dogs spend around us, the more they seem to become more than just an animal. In fact, your dog will become adept at recognizing and interpreting human behavior—especially yours—and will not think of itself as a different species, but merely as part of your "pack." The idea of wearing costumes is therefore not so completely alien to a canine as you might think. It will have observed you wearing different clothes every day, and as anyone who has ever bought a doggie coat will tell you, dogs quickly and easily get used to wearing garments to keep out the cold—and are quite comfortable in them. To a dog, there is no difference between a warming coat and an Elvis Presley outfit. As long as its movement is not impeded and the outfit does not make the dog uncomfortable or overly warm, you can dress up your pet however you like. It may take a little while for the pooch to get used to the strange sensation of wearing a costume, but once it has, it will thoroughly enjoy being the center of attention and feeling like a part of the group.

There is a long tradition of dressing dogs in ruffs and hats that stretches back to the heyday of the circus, but for this book, we have gone just a little further to highlight outfits that either complement the breed of dog or in some way reflect their personalities or the lives of their owners. For example, Buddy—the dog in the Elvis outfit on page 73—is owned by a well-known singer who is currently working in Reno, while Hector on page 18 is a French bulldog who lives with the owner of the water garden in France from which the painter Monet once bought the lilies in his famous paintings. Of course, we have also added a few seasonal costumes—Halloween and Christmas, for instance—and a couple that might seem to have no particular relevance, but are suited to the personality of the dog. Liquorice on page 34 may look like the most adorable puppy, but there is very good reason for him to be dressed as a devil!

There are many different dog breeds out there, and we have tried to include a range of costumes for dogs big and small, as well as for people with a range of crafting and needlework ability. Some outfits are very simple and can be made by anyone with a needle, thread, and a few minutes on their hands while others are a little more complicated and might require some patience.

A few words of advice before you start dressing up your dog: Always double-check that you have removed all pins and that there are no sharp corners on the outfit that might harm your dog. If this is the first time the dog has worn any outfit, it will probably be a little nervous at first, so begin with a simple costume and use treats to coax him or her into it. If after ten minutes or so it becomes obvious that the dog is not enjoying the experience, take the costume off and wait a while before trying again. For this reason, it is worth having your dog get used to a costume before its grand appearance at a party. Lastly, there are few things in life so cute or funny as a well-dressed dog, so use your imagination and don't be afraid to adapt the ideas in this book for your own designs.

The author would like to thank the following for kindly lending their dogs as models:

Greg and Monica London (Buddy)

Trish and John Wall (Abi)

Terry and Sandra Lubbock (Ollie)

Phee and Danny McCarthy (Muddles and Sophie)

Sue and Ken Napier (Tessa)

Carina and David Penney (Angel, Susie, Lily, Josh, Scooby)

Martin Howard (Satch and Licky)

Jenny and Brian Ayling (Nahla)

Robin and Celia Harhy (Whisper)

Annechien and Clive Smith (Polly)

Val and Brian Levy (Archie)

Robert Sheldon (Hector)

Julian and Nikki Garafano (Boogie)

EQUIPMENT

Although all of the following costumes are easy to make, there are a few basic materials and tools that you will need. Each project includes a materials list, but you will also need the following items.

Sewing machine

Any good-quality sewing machine is a joy to use, saving hours of hand-sewing and giving a professional finish to all your crafts. Ensure that you have the correct-sized needle for your fabric and the right tension or size of stitch. Also, buy a quality thread (polyester is strong and washable).

Scissors

It is important to use a pair of good, sharp scissors that have been used only for cutting fabrics. If you try to cut material with blunt or damaged scissors, they will not give you a good edge to your pattern pieces. For tips on clipping curves and corners, see p. 96.

Tape measure

The measurements in this book have been made with a fabric measure.

Pins

Use pins with a round, colored head, as they are easy to hold and, should they drop onto the floor, are easy to find.

Iron and ironing board

You will give your costumes a professional finish if you iron the seams as you go. Be sure to set the iron at the correct temperature for your fabric.

Glue gun

This is not an essential item for the costumes in this book, but will speed up projects such as the angel wings. I would recommend a small model with a low temperature setting.

Craft knife

A craft knife will be useful to cut out the "Super Dog" emblem and the feathers of the angel costume to size. These extremely sharp blades should be kept well away from dogs and children. Always work on a cutting board, cut away from your body, and store the knife in a safe place. You will find that the blade can be made safe when pushed into the middle of a cheap pencil eraser.

Sewing terms

Tacking: fairly long running stitches done by hand.

Machine stitching: a medium stitch done on a sewing machine. (If you don't have a sewing machine, this can be done by hand.)

Overstitch: stitching together two pieces of fabric by hand, going through both pieces of material close to the edge with small stitches close together, and taking the thread over the top of both pieces of fabric.

Hem: to hem, turn under a raw edge to the wrong side of the material, press, and turn over again. Press again and stitch down.

Seam: two pieces of material sewn together with the right sides of material facing, pinned together, and sewn at the given measurement from the edges. Press open unless otherwise stated.

Hand stitch: small stitches using a needle and thread.

Gathering stitch or Ease-stitch: a machine stitch just above the seam using long machine stitches that can be gently pulled when adjusting to fit.

Topstitch: stitching on the right side close to the seam or previous stitching.

Wire and wire cutters

A medium-sized wire covered in white plastic is lightweight and bends easily. A pair of wire cutters saves time and effort, and gives a good, clean cut. Make sure that the ends of the wire are secured safely to avoid causing any harm to the dog.

Something pointy!

For turning out bands, belts, and pointy things, a thin stick or long pencil is very helpful.

HINTS AND TIPS

- Before you begin making your dog's costume, cut out the pattern pieces in paper or cheap material to determine whether it will be a good fit for your dog. Measuring your dog carefully is crucial to the success of your costume, and there is a list below of the measurements you will need.

  Around the neck

  Back of neck to tail

  Around chest

  Around waist

  Width across the front

  Floor to floor over dog's back

  Between the ears

  Length of tail

- Taking your time when cutting out patterns in material may save you from having to start over. Before cutting, check that the pattern piece does not need to be on a fold or an edge, and that you have allowed enough material for your seams.

- Pressing the seams as you go along gives your outfit a professional finish, as does completing each garment by trimming loose threads.

- When turning out shapes and curves in the fabric, take time to clip away corners and excess material first to get the best finish, making sure, of course, to not cut the stitching. Tease out the pointy parts with a pin or tweezers.

- To pin two pieces of material together, it is best to point the pins in toward the edge of the fabric. This allows you to sew your seam without taking the pins out, and also helps the fabric to lay flat.

- Choose fabrics carefully. The stretchy kind can be difficult to sew, while cotton and satin make sewing much easier—and are also a little more dog-proof.

- To cut out a circle in a piece of material—for example, leg holes—first snip a small hole in the center, then cut across the diameter, both horizontally and vertically, creating an "x." This makes it easier to cut the circle.

- There are several different thicknesses of iron-on stiffener, and for most of these costumes a medium grade will do, but do not use the heavy-duty weight unless otherwise stated, as it will make your medium grade material too stiff. Once the sticky side is facing the material (it is usually shinier on the sticky side), always begin ironing from the middle and work outward in order to prevent air pockets from forming.

- The drawings in this book are not to scale, but are meant to assist you in creating your own patterns. You can use a photocopier to enlarge the images to the size of your dog, which should make a good starting point.

Confidence and safety

- Always ensure that all pins are removed from the costume when you have finished. You do not want to use your pet as a pincushion! Check the floor around your work area as pins can easily become stuck in paws.

- If your dog is likely to be near any kind of flame (barbecues or candles, for example), be sure the material is flame-resistant before you buy it.

- When tying ribbon around your dog's neck, make sure that the dog is comfortable and able to breathe easily.

- To help with your dog's confidence and willingness to wear a costume, allow the dog to smell it before you attempt to put it on. Lay the outfit over the dog's back and encourage it with positive words and maybe a small treat. Gradually put a part of the costume on, always being positive with the animal, allowing it to understand that it is not a threat but something that pleases you. Continue with this training until the dog allows you to dress it without a struggle.

- While every effort has been made to make these costumes comfortable and safe for your animals, do not leave your dog unattended while it is wearing one.

RAPPER

This outfit is one of the easiest in the book to make, consisting of a T-shirt, baseball cap, and lots of "gold" chains. The baseball cap could be made, but why bother when a child's size can be bought from a store for about the same amount as the cost of the fabric? The chains were also found in a store and were inexpensive. Try not to buy heavy chains, but since Scooby is a big, strong cross between a Newfoundland and a Gordon setter, he was not distressed by them. Should yours be a smaller breed, then perhaps just one or two chains would be sufficient. This of course leaves only the T-shirt to make—and what could be easier? This particular shirt is of a soft, slightly stretchy camouflage material that does not fray, but feel free to experiment. For additional accessories, you could make fake sunglasses from black cardboard to add to the hat.

Materials

For a large dog
2¹/₂ ft. camouflage material
5 ft. bias binding of a similar color

1 ft. Velcro fastening
Child's baseball hat
Gold chains

1 Cut out the shirt back and the two pieces of shirt front and make two small darts on either side of the shirt back at the neck edge.

2 Make a small dart on each front piece at the center of the neck edge, then pin the shirt fronts to the shirt back, right sides of material facing, and stitch the side and underarm seams. Clip the underarm corners and press the seams open.

3 Pin the fronts and back together at the shoulder edges, right sides of material facing, and stitch across the shoulder edges. Press the seams open. Neaten the lower edge and the sleeve edges with small hems. Make a hem on the underside of the T-shirt, leaving enough material to overlap the two edges under your dog's chest.

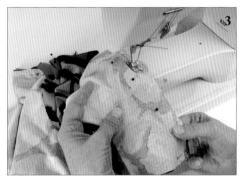

4 Neaten the neck edge with soft bias binding of the same color as your T-shirt. Pin the bias binding to the right side of the neck edge and stitch. Fold the binding over to the wrong side and hand stitch it into place, neatening the ends.

5 Finish the T-shirt by sewing Velcro to the underside hems to fasten.

PIERROT

A Pierrot is an extremely simple yet effective costume that looks particularly good on a black or white dog like Boogie the Dalmation. It is extremely easy to make, being just a ruff and a hat, and is rather versatile. For example, it can be adapted to make many other fancy costumes—such as a pixie, gnome, or clown—just by using colorful fabrics. For dogs who are not too sure about dressing up, this is one of the more comfortable to wear and difficult to dislodge. For best results, use firm fabrics such as cotton or satin for the ruff because softer materials like nylon tend to droop and look sad.

Materials

For a large dog

Black material measuring 5 ft. x 8 in.	10 in. white felt
White material measuring 5 ft. x 6½ in.	10 in. black felt
5 ft. white rickrack trimming	10 in. iron-on stiffening
5 ft. black rickrack trimming	1 ball thick white wool
5 ft. white bias binding ¾ in. wide	1 ball thick black wool
1 yd. white ribbon ¼-½ in. wide	Small piece of black elastic
or 1 yd. soft elastic	Black and white cotton
	Safety pin

1 To make the ruff, turn over ¼ inch on the long edge of the black material to the wrong side, pin, and press flat. Turn it under again, pin, and sew to make a ¼-inch hem. Press it flat. Do the same again on the white material to neaten one long edge.

2 On the right side of the black hem, pin and stitch the white trimming. Be careful not to pull the trimming tight or it will make the hem buckle. Trim the right side of the hem of the white fabric with the black trimming.

3 Place both pieces of the black and white material together on the long, unhemmed edge, making sure that the right side of the white material is facing the wrong side of the black. Sew a ¼-inch seam and press the seam open. Neaten both of the short ends of the joined material with a small hem.

4 Place the bias binding right side up to the wrong side of the center seam, turning the ends under at each end to neaten. Pin and stitch down each side, leaving the ends open to form a channel to place the ribbon.

5 Attach the safety pin to the ribbon and slide through the channel, leaving some of the ribbon free on the ends. Adjust the length of the ruff to suit the dog's neck and secure the ribbon at each end to keep the ribbon from disappearing into the channel. If you would rather use elastic, measure a piece to the size of your dog's neck plus ½ inch and thread through the channel with the safety pin. Secure the two ends of the elastic together.

6 To make the hat, cut out one pattern piece in white felt, one in black felt, and two pattern pieces in iron-on stiffening. Iron the stiffening to one side of each. Pin the two pieces of the hat together, right sides facing, and stitch them together.

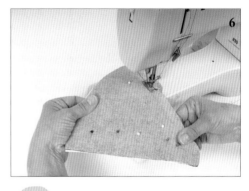

7 Turn the hat right side out, turn a small hem to the inside of the hat at the bottom edge, and stitch to neaten and strengthen.

8 Make one white and one black pom-pom as follows. Cut out two pieces of stiff cardboard 4 inches by 1½ inches and place them together with a long piece of wool between them. (This is to later tie up the pom-pom and sew it onto the hat.) Wind the wool over the two pieces of cardboard until it is quite thick, being careful to keep the long pieces of wool free. Cut along one of the edges through all of the wool and tie into a ball with the long piece of wool that was initially placed in the middle of the cardboard. Tie it up very tightly, trim, and sew to the hat.

9 Measure a piece of elastic under your dog's chin and sew each end to the middle of the bottom edge of each color.

FRENCHMAN

Hector is a young French bulldog who lives with his American owner in a picturesque water lily garden in the south of France. He is a very French dog who lives in a very French location (the gardens are famous for having supplied Monet with the lilies featured in his paintings), so this outfit seemed apropos. He is wearing a blue-and-white-striped T-shirt, red scarf, and—of course—the traditional black beret. A string of small onions would be a great addition if you can trust your dog not to chew them! For the T-shirt, a stretchy, striped material was used, allowing freedom of movement. Make sure to cut it so that the stripes go across horizontally, as the French would wear.

Materials

For a small dog

1½ ft. blue-and-white-striped material

Piece of black felt 10 in. square

Iron-on stiffening 10 in. square

2 ft. red fabric

1½ ft. white bias binding

10 in. black bias binding

White Velcro fastening

1 To make the beret, cut out a circle in black felt. (A large tea plate serves as a good pattern.) Iron on the lightweight stiffener, then gather the outside edge so that the felt turns to the inside.

2 Pin the black bias binding to the gathered felt and stitch them together. Fold the bias binding to the underneath of the felt and hand stitch to neaten.

3 Roll the small piece of black felt to form the beret detail, and stitch it together, then stitch it onto the hat so that it sticks up into the air. To finish, sew a piece of elastic underneath the hat on either side to fit under your dog's chin comfortably.

4 Cut out the shirt back and the two pieces of the shirt front and make two small darts on either side of the shirt back at the neck edge (see diagram). Make a small dart on each front piece at the center of the neck edge.

5 Pin both of the shirt fronts to the shirt back, right sides of material facing, and stitch the side and underarm seams. Clip the underarm corners and press the seams open.

6 Pin the fronts and back together at the shoulder edges, right sides of material facing, and stitch across the shoulder edges. Press the seams open.

7 Neaten the lower edge and the sleeve edges with small hems.

8 Neaten the neck edge with either a simple hem or soft bias binding. Pin the bias binding to the right side of the neck edge and stitch. Fold the binding over to the wrong side and pin, then hand stitch into place, ensure you have enough length each side to tie around your dog's neck, and neaten the ends. Make a hem on the underside of the T-shirt,

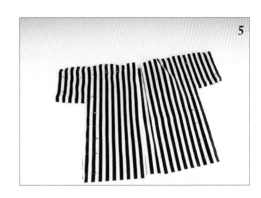

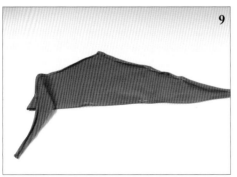

leaving enough material to overlap under your dog's chest. Sew Velcro to the underside hems to fasten.

9 Cut out the triangular scarf shape in red material and hem around all sides with a small hem. Press well and cut off any hanging threads. *Voilà*, the costume is finished.

HIPPIE

Muddles is an easygoing brown spaniel who looks like a hippie with his long, hairy ears and sleepy eyes, so he seemed a great candidate to model this quick and easy-to-make costume, which consists of a shirt, beads, and a tie for the head. To make the shirt, use a colorful cotton fabric, preferably tie-dyed in a sixties manner, or any material that looks psychedelic. If you like, you can decorate the back of the shirt with a peace symbol. You will also need some colorful beads and a flower to finish it all off.

Materials

For a medium dog

1½ ft. colorful material

1 yd. bias binding

A small piece of white felt

10 in. black ribbon

1 yd. ribbon to match your material

Some colorful beads to fit your dog's neck

A simple flower

1 Cut out the shirt back and the two pieces of shirt front. Make two small darts on either side of the shirt back at the neck edge. Make a small dart on each front piece at the center of the neck edge.

2 Pin shirt fronts to shirt back, right sides of material facing, and stitch side and underarm seams. Clip the underarm corner and press seams open. Pin fronts and back together at the shoulder edges, right sides of material facing, and stitch across the shoulder edges. Press seam open.

3 Neaten lower edge and arm holes with a small hem. Also make a hem on the underside of the shirt, leaving enough material to overlap the two edges.

4 Finish the neck edge with bias binding. Pin the bias binding to the right side of the neck edge, leaving enough to tie into a bow at each side. Stitch the bias binding to the shirt, then fold over to the wrong side and hand stitch into place. Fold the tie pieces of the binding in half and stitch together.

5 Sew Velcro to the underside hems to fasten.

6 Decorate your shirt with a peace symbol, made with a white felt circle and black ribbon or bias binding.

7 To make the headband, cut a strip of material three inches wide and long enough to tie around your dog's head. Make a knot and hang loose. Fold the material in half lengthwise, right side of material facing out, pin, and sew across one end and along the length. Leave the other end open to turn out. Clip the corner. Turn out to the right side, then turn under the open end and sew the edges together. Press flat.

8 Sew a flower onto the tie so that it will be on the side of the dog's head when it is tied.

A SIMPLE WITCH

Perfect for Halloween, this witch costume—modeled by Nahla—is very easy to make and easy for any dog to wear. If you want to be a little more colorful, it could easily become a wizard's outfit by using gold, purple, or green fabric (perhaps with some stars and moons sewn on), but black is simple as well as traditional for witches. The costume consists of a cloak and a hat, made in felt because it is soft and comfortable for the dog. If it gets a bit battered—as is likely if you have an enthusiastic dog—then it will look all the more authentic. A small buckle can be cut out of cardboard and some sequined braid, or any kind of ribbon will do to decorate it. The cloak has been lined in green to match the ribbon, but an even simpler version can be made by just hemming a single piece of black fabric.

Materials

For a large dog

1 yd. black material

1 yd. lining material in whatever color you
    prefer (optional)

1 yd. black bias binding ³⁄₄ in. wide

1 yd. black ribbon ¹⁄₄ to ³⁄₄ in. wide

16 in. black felt

16 in. iron-on stiffening

Piece of black elastic to fit under dog's chin

1 small buckle or cardboard to cut out (optional)

20 in. ribbon for hat to match lining (optional)

Black cotton

Decorations such as stars, moon, etc. (optional)

1 To make the hat, cut out two felt circles 8 inches in diameter and one circle of iron-on stiffening of the same size. Place the shiny side of the stiffener onto one of the felt circles and iron down. Pin both of the black circles together, then sew around the brim close to the edge, leaving a gap of about 2 inches to turn it right side out.

2 Turn the brim right side out, press flat, and sew up the gap. To strengthen it, machine stitch again around the brim close to the edge.

3 Cut out two pieces of the crown in felt, then cut out the same pattern in iron-on stiffening twice. Iron the stiffening to both pieces of the felt, then place both pieces of felt together and stitch around the pointed shape of the crown close to the edge. Cut away any extra material at the top. Turn the crown right side out, gently easing out the pointed top part.

4 Cut slits around the lower edge of the crown by 1/8 inch and turn under to the inside.

5 Pin the crown to the brim, keeping it as equal as possible all around. Sew the crown and the brim together, then decorate.

6 To make the cloak, measure your dog along its back from the nape of its neck to the beginning of its tail, and add 4 inches for the collar. This will give you the depth of material needed. Measure over the dog's back on each side from floor to floor, and this will be the material width.

Cut a piece of black material (see pattern) and—if you wish—another piece the same size in the lining material of your choice. Place lining on a flat surface, right side up, then match black material on top, right side down, so that the right sides are facing together on the inside. Pin together.

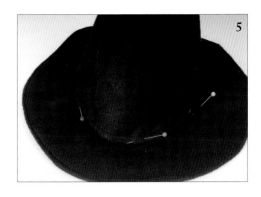

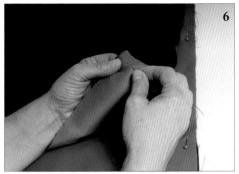

7 Sew all around the material, leaving an opening of about 3 inches to pull material through. The seam should be about ½ inch from the edge. Take out all the pins, clip the excess material at corners, and ease material through the opening, making sure that all the material—including the corners—is right side out. Press it flat and sew up the open edge. For a simple version, just hem your black cloak all around.

8 On the lining side of material (or the hemmed side), measure a straight line 4 inches away from the top edge to allow for a raised collar. This will become the neck edge.

9 On this line, pin a strip of tape or bias binding, then turn under both edges of the tape at either end. Sew bias binding close to both edges, leaving the ends open to thread the ribbon through.

10 Using a safety pin attached to one end of the ribbon, thread ribbon through the channel in the bias binding until you reach the middle of the cloak, then pin the ribbon that is still free at the end you started to the binding so that it cannot pull through. Now push the rest of the ribbon through the channel (it will now start gathering) and pull it out the other end.

11 Adjust the gathers until they measure about a quarter of the original width of the cloak and it fits the dog's neck comfortably, making sure that the ribbon is equal lengths on both ends, leaving enough ribbon on each end for tying. Cut off any loose ends, press, and finish off by decorating as you wish.

FLOWER

This simple flower costume consists of a collar made up of two rows of different-colored petals on a green band, with a little daisy hat to match. The petals can be made in any range of colors to suit your dog. Felt is easiest to use, soft to wear, quite durable, and does not fray. For small dogs, use small petals, and for a larger dog, increase both the size and number of them. Lily—our aptly named flower model—is a little Yorkshire terrier full of character and energy.

Materials

For a small dog

10 in. white felt

10 in. green felt

10 in. yellow felt

A small piece of Velcro

A small piece of thin elastic to fit under your dog's chin

Green sewing cotton (optional)

1. To make the flower collar, measure your dog's neck and add 1½ inches for fastening, then cut out a band at the above measurement 3 inches wide. Also cut out seven white petals and six smaller petals.

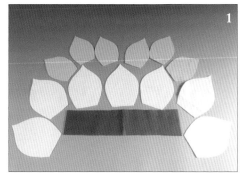

2. Fold all the petals as shown above by making a pleat on each side. Pin and tack them in place.

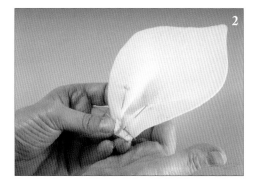

3. Pin the white petals, evenly spaced, along the top of the band, leaving ¾ inch at each end free for fastening. Tack them in place.

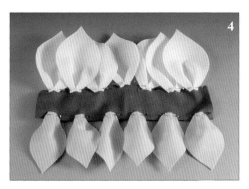

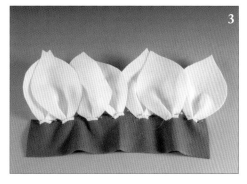

4. Pin the lower edge of the yellow petals face down onto the bottom edge of the band, then tack them down.

5. Fold the band in half lengthwise so that the lower edges of the petals are inside the band. Pin and stitch around all the outside edges of the band.

Dress Up Your Dog **29**

6 Sew the Velcro to each end to allow the band to stretch comfortably around your dog's neck. Remove all tacking.

7 To make the hat, cut out two green leaf shapes, six small white petals, and two yellow circles. Using a large machine stitch, sew along the bottom of all the white petals, one after the other, so that they are all in a line. Gather them to fit inside the yellow circle.

8 Place the two yellow circles together and hand stitch them over the white petals to join them all together. This will make the yellow center slightly raised.

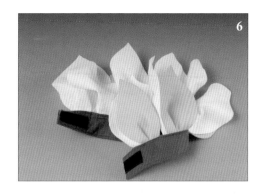

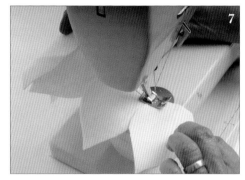

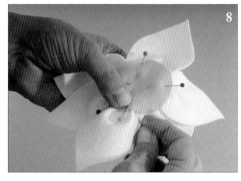

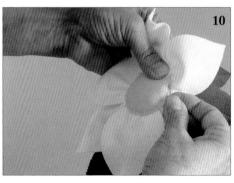

9 Stitch together the two leaf shapes and machine stitch leaf spines down the leaves to strengthen them and add realistic design.

10 Sew the flower onto the leaves, allowing some of the leaves to be seen, then attach thin elastic to fit comfortably under your dog's chin.

ANGEL

Not all costumes need laborious cutting and sewing. This is a project that makes the most of the dog's natural appearance and adds a couple of simple details—a pair of wings and a halo—to turn any pup into a heavenly angel. The costume consists of a swansdown halo and a feathery pair of wings. If you cannot find swansdown for the halo, then bind it in gold ribbon or gold bias binding, which will look just as attractive. Equally, if you cannot find real feathers, or just want to use household products, feather shapes cut from white paper will be fine. In fact, you could make the wings from cardboard covered with paper feathers if you wanted. If your dog is a darker color, then you might want to make some bat wings instead, especially around Halloween. Our model for this costume is a beautiful white Swiss alsatian puppy—aptly named Angel—who is just eight weeks old.

Materials

For a small or medium dog

A child's white plastic headband

White plastic-coated wire

A small piece of swansdown trimming or
gold ribbon

1 ft. white material (such as felt)

1 ft. iron-on heavy-duty stiffener

1 ft. white batting

2 ft. white bias binding or white tape

2 pieces of wire the width across the two wings

2 large bags of white feathers

Glue and glue gun

White ribbon

Velcro for fastening

1 To make the halo, shape the white wire into a double circle, then wrap the wire around the circles to hold them together. Using the same wire, make a straight piece, then loop the end around the child's headband and bring it up, wrapping it around the straight piece back to the circles, and finish it off by looping the end of the wire around the circles to hold in place.

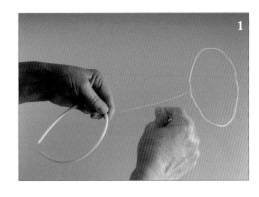

2 Cover and bind the plastic headpiece and straight piece in the satin bias binding, stitching it in place at the ends to prevent it from unwinding.

3 Attach the swansdown to the halo using a winding movement with the white wire or strong cotton.

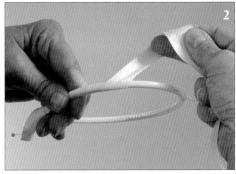

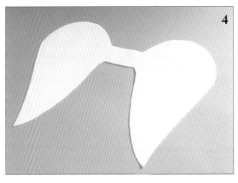

4 Cut out the wing shapes in felt, iron-on stiffening, and batting. Iron the stiffening onto the felt.

5 Pin the bias binding across the two wings and the middle band, then sew across one end and down both long sides.

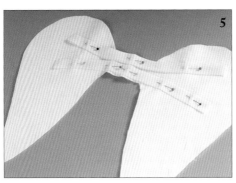

6 Push the wires into the channel of the bias binding and sew up the open ends.

7 Glue the batting over the two wings and the center piece on the side of the wires.

8 Glue feathers onto the felt side of the wings, imitating as far as possible the direction of a bird's feathers. Also glue the smallest feathers down the edge of the batting. When the glue has dried, bend the wires gently up on each side of the center piece. (The batting will go to the inside of the wing.)

9 Cut a band of felt 3 inches wide and long enough to fit over the center part of the wings, and around the dog's collar with enough spare to fold over and Velcro together.

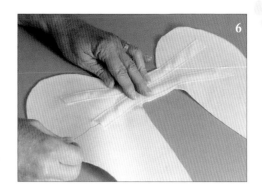

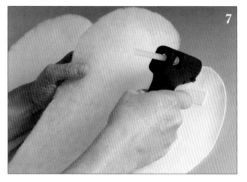

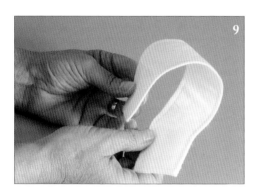

Fold the width in half, pin together, and stitch all around each edge. Finish by stitching a piece of Velcro to each end of the band.

10 The wings will be fastened by putting the band around the center band of the wings and your dog's collar, and sewing a ribbon on which can be tied under the dog's chest.

DEVIL

Liquorice, or "Licky" as he's usually known, is a rescue dog and—although he's very cute—is such a troublemaker that a devil costume immediately came to mind when outfitting him. This costume in bright red and orange is fairly simple already, but can be made even more so. The tailpiece can be omitted (it's not recommended for a dog with a bushy tail) and the over-cape can be left off too. Here, the cape is lined with orange fabric, but the lining is optional, as are the sparkly embellishments. This costume could also be easily adapted into a court jester outfit by wearing it orange side out and making a hat using four horn shapes (two red and two orange) sewn onto a small circle with the horns pointing outward (instead of inward like a devil's horns) and finished with small bells.

Materials

For a small or medium dog

2¹/₂ ft. red fabric

2¹/₂ ft. orange fabric

Small amount of stuffing for the horns and tailpiece

Red cotton

Sequins and glue for sequins (optional)

Tiny piece of iron-on stiffening for headpiece

Elastic to fit under your dog's chin

A small piece of Velcro

Before you begin, make a paper pattern for each piece of the cape, both of which need to be cut out on the fold. Fold the red material on one side to fit the depth of the cape and pin the paper shape to the fold and around the flames. Fold up other end to fit the over-cape shape, and pin to the fold and around the flame shapes. Pin two horn shapes (four pieces are needed) and the hat base (two pieces are needed) to this piece of material and cut out all pieces. On the remaining middle piece of red material, pin the tail shape and cut out. In the same way, cut out the cape and over-cape lining from the orange material.

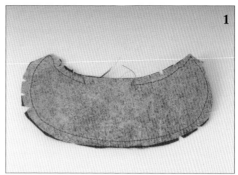

1 To make the horned headpiece, cut out the hat base from the iron-on stiffening and iron onto the wrong side of one hat base piece. Place both hat pieces together, right sides facing, pin, and sew close to the edge,

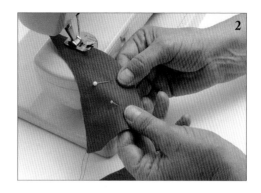

leaving an opening of about 1 inch on the longest back edge to turn out. Trim off excess material at the corners, clip the curves, and ease right side out. Sew up the opening, and press.

2 Make the horns by putting two pieces together, right sides facing, pin, and sew close to the edge. Cut off excess fabric at the top of horn, clip curves, and turn right side out. Make another in the same method.

3 Fill the horns tightly with stuffing, pushing it into the top of the horn with a pencil.

4 Turn under the lower edges, pin, and hand sew to the hat piece. Decorate with sequins, if desired. Attach elastic to fit comfortably under your dog's chin.

5 To make the cape, place the red upper cape piece and the orange lining piece together, right sides facing.

6 Pin and carefully stitch around all cape edges, leaving an opening to turn out. Trim away excess material at the flame points and corners, clip curves (take time with this, as it will help make the curved flames more successful), and turn out gently, easing points out with a pin. Stitch up the opening and press flat, again easing the shapes out as you press. Then make the larger cape piece in the same way.

7 Slipstitch the smaller top cape to the main cape on the red side, matching neck centers, and sew Velcro on the tabs at the neck edge, and at the back if you plan to make a tailpiece.

8 Make the straps to fasten under the dog's stomach by placing the strap pieces together, right sides of material facing. Pin, then stitch down one end and along the side, leaving an end open to turn out. Clip the corners and turn out to the right side. Press and stitch the open ends.

9 Sew Velcro onto both straps, taking care that the Velcro with the hooks goes to the bottom piece of the strap so that it will not catch in the dog's fur as easily. Place straps to each side of the cloak to fit your dog's waist and stitch them to the underside of the cloak.

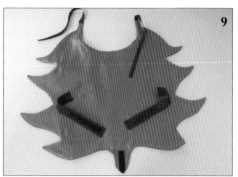

10 To make the tailpiece, neaten the top edge of fabric with a small hem, then fold the tail in half lengthwise, pin, and stitch it down near to the edge. Trim off the excess fabric at the tip, take out the pins, and turn it out. Make the tail tip by placing both pieces of heart shape together, right sides of material facing, then stitch it along the edges, leaving an opening to turn it out to the right side.

11 Clip the curves and corners, then turn the tail tip right side out, fill with batting, and sew up the open edge. Sew the tip to the other tailpiece, making sure that the seam is underneath, and attach the finished tailpiece to the cape using Velcro. You can now decorate the costume with sequins if you like.

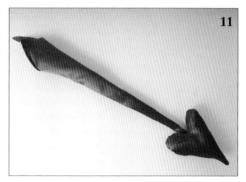

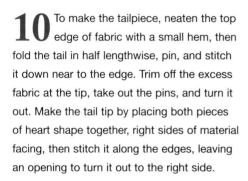

MONK

For this relatively simple costume, you can use any dark brown fabric, so long as it is not too thin. This particular fabric looks like suede, but is lightweight and will not make the dog too hot (especially since he already has a heavy coat). It is also easy to sew and does not fray. The outfit consists of a cowl and robe, and is completed with a wooden rosary, which can be made simply by threading wooden beads onto a strong thread, with a knot between each. If you can find or make a wooden cross, this really helps to finish the costume. Our model is Ollie, a big, gentle Bernese mountain dog who suits the monk outfit perfectly.

Materials

For a large dog

5 ft. brown material

Brown cotton for sewing

Small wooden beads

Thin twine or strong thread

Small cross

1. To make the robe, cut out both pieces of the pattern in your chosen material at a suitable size to fit your dog and neaten the outside edge of neck facing with a tiny hem on the wrong side.

2. Place the neck facing to the robe neck, right sides of material facing, pin, and stitch making a ¼-inch seam. Clip the curves, taking care not to cut through the seam line, and press open.

3. With right sides of material together, pin the robe and facing under the neck, then sew them together making a ¼-inch seam. Turn out the neck facing at the neck edge, then turn all facing down to the wrong side and press flat.

4. Stitch around neck edge over material and facing. Tack facing to robe at seams to hold flat.

5. With right sides of material together and sewing a ¼-inch seam, stitch the back edge of robe together, leaving a large opening for your dog's tail to come through, then neaten the tail opening with a small hem. Turn under the lower edge of robe and machine stitch.

6 To make the cowl, cut out the back and side pieces as in the diagram, measured for your dog, and place each side piece to the back piece, right sides of material together, pin, and stitch. Press the seam open.

6

7 Fold the cowl in half, right sides of material together, and pin along the top edge. Machine stitch them together, making a ¹/₄-inch seam.

7

8

8 Pin and stitch one-third of the front opening, leaving two-thirds open for your dog's face. Press the seam open. Neaten the edges of the front opening with a small hem, then hem the lower edge and press. Finish by cutting off any loose threads and press well.

9

9 String wooden beads onto a piece of twine or thread big enough to hang around your dog's neck, placing a wooden cross in the middle. A simple cross can be made with two sticks tied together across the middle.

HAWAIIAN GIRL

This costume is very easy to make and would look good on any dog, particularly for a summer barbecue. It can be as colorful as you like, and made in most fabrics, but cotton is easy both to use and wash. If you cannot find raffia to make the skirt, then wool or strips of strong brown paper will work. Our model is a Basenji named Polly, who comes from Crufts champion stock.

Materials

For a small or medium dog

1½ ft. brightly colored material for bikini
   top and skirt band

Raffia, wool, or sturdy brown paper for skirt

Colorful fabric, tissue, or crepe paper for flowers

Plastic tubular beads or thin straws

Strong thread

Elastic (enough to go around your dog's chest twice)

Small piece of brightly colored ribbon

Velcro

1 To make the skirt, cut out a band of colorful material approxmately 3 inches wide, long enough to go around your dog's stomach, plus 2 inches for seams and overlap. Cut a piece of iron-on stiffening the same size. Iron on the stiffening to the band material (wrong side).

2 Turn under material to the wrong side, ½ inch at the bottom of each length. Press flat.

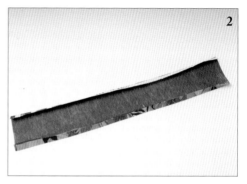

3 Fold the material in half, right side of material facing, and sew down each width end, leaving the longer length edges open to tuck the raffia into.

4 Fold the raffia strips in half, tuck the folded edges into the open length of the band, pin the ends together, and machine

stitch into place a little at a time. Sew on Velcro to fasten under your dog's waist.

5 To make the bikini top, cut out a piece of the brightly colored material as shown in the diagram. Make a hem ½ inch on each end.

6 Fold the material in half lengthwise, right sides of material together, pin, and stitch a seam ½ inch wide. You should now have a tube of material.

7 With the seam in the middle of the band, turn the material right side out and press it flat. This will be the wrong side of the bikini top. Make a channel for the elastic by sewing a seam ½ inch away from each folded edge. Leave the ends of the channel open, but hand stitch the middle part of the fabric together at each end.

8 Cut two pieces of elastic to fit comfortably around the chest of your dog, and, with a safety pin, thread the elastic through each channel, pinning it at each end to secure. Stitch the elastic into place at each end.

9 Sew a piece of Velcro at each end to fasten under your dog's chest. Mark the midpoint of the band with a pin, then decorate with a loop of ribbon and a brightly colored bow or a flower.

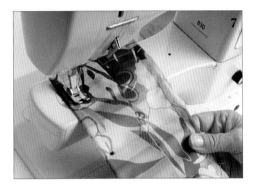

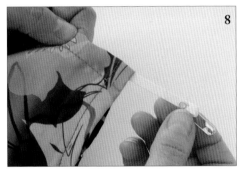

10 To make the lei, cut about fifty flower shapes from a single color or use many different colors if preferred. With a strong thread, begin to make the lei by tying a piece of straw or tubular bead to the end, leaving some thread free to tie up the other end. Attach the other end to a needle and thread two or three flowers and a straw bead alternately. When the lei is long enough to go around your dog's neck, knot the string together to form a lei.

CLEOPATRA

For my own dog, Ella, I made a fancy Cleopatra dress in turquoise, gold, blue, and black, inspired by the Egyptian-like markings around Ella's eyes and her regal attitude. This costume can be as sumptuous or as simple as you like, and is made up of a simple coat and collar with a snake headdress. If you want to simplify it, then the collar and headdress alone would be sufficient to suggest ancient Egypt. The collar was designed using a basic dinner plate. For a small dog, use a salad plate. We recommend making it in newspaper first to fit and adjust on your own dog. Measure around your dog's neck to find the exact inner-neck size.

Materials

For a medium dog

5 ft. turquoise material	Thin and medium wire
2½ ft. interlining (optional)	Wire cutters
Gold and black braid or ribbon for trimming	White tape
Velcro for fastening cape and collar	10 in. batting cut into thin strips
1½ ft. gold material	Turquoise satin bias binding
2½ ft. iron-on stiffening	Narrow gold braid
Turquoise, black, and royal blue trimming	Two black beads or sequins for eyes

Cut out the fabric before you begin. Measure around your dog's waist, add 1½ inches for overlap and 1 inch for seams—the width for cutting out the coat. Measure the length of your dog from the nape of its neck to the start of its tail, and add 1 inch for the seam. This is the length for cutting. You should now have a rectangle of material the correct length and width. Fold the width of the material in half and mark the center with a pin. Cut two pieces of material as shown in the diagram and a piece in interlining (optional).

1 If you are using interlining, tack it to the wrong side of the coat material, then pin the lining material to the coat, right sides of material facing. Sew around all edges ½ inch from the edge, leaving an opening at one end to pull the material right side out. Clip the

inner corners and cut surplus material from the outer corners.

2 Turn out to the right side, turn under the opening, and stitch together to neaten. Sew on Velcro to fasten under the dog's stomach.

3 To finish, decorate with gold fabric, braid, or sequins, and sew Velcro to the neck end of the coat to attach it to the collar.

4 To make the collar, cut out the collar shape twice in gold material. Cut two pieces in iron-on stiffening. Iron stiffening on to the wrong sides of the gold shapes. Place the gold material together, right sides of material facing, and sew around collar near the edge, leaving an opening to turn out.

5 Turn the material right side out, shaping the corners, turn under the edges of the opening, then hand sew the unstitched edges together. Press it well, and sew on Velcro at the ends of the collar, which will fasten to the piece on the jacket.

6 Decorate as desired.

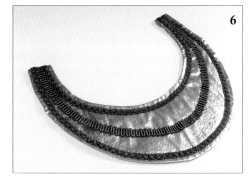

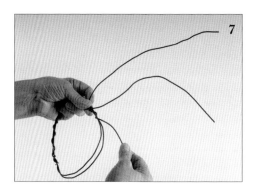

7 To make the snake headdress, form a double circle of flexible wire to fit your dog's head between its ears, leaving two pieces of wire long enough to fashion a curved snake. Coil another piece of wire around the two circles to secure and strengthen.

8 Bind the headdress with more thin wire, leaving enough at the top to fashion the thick wire into a snake's head and fangs.

9 To form the head of the snake, place two pieces of batting at the top of the wire and bind into place, tightening and loosening the binding to make the shape.

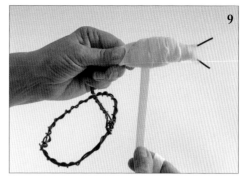

10 Cut some strips of batting and wrap over the wire, then tape in place with soft bias binding or thin strips of material.

11 Now take the turquoise satin bias binding and wind it around all of the headdress, tacking as you go to hold it in place. Bind again in gold braid, leaving some of the turquoise binding showing. Bring the gold braid over the head of the snake and form a V shape.

12 Tack braid into place, then finish by sewing on two black beads for eyes. Stitch elastic to each side of the base of the headdress to fit under your dog's chin.

PRINCESS

This costume is a dream to make—simple but effective. Let your imagination run wild and use as much or as little embellishment as you like. We have used a pink fabric that stands out in any crowd and lots of mesh for the skirt. Bows, braid, and sequins finish it off nicely. It can be made in any color and could—if you prefer—include wings sewn onto the back. Sophie, our Maltese terrier, looks lovely in her costume. This was made for a small dog but would look good on almost any breed. For a larger dog, scale up the measurements. Start by measuring around your dog's stomach, taking the widest part, and adding 2 inches for seams and fastening. Then measure the length of the back, from neck to tail. Remember to check height from the floor when cutting out the mesh skirt or it may touch the floor. Use half of this neck-to-tail measurement for the skirt and half for the top. For the straps, measure from the dog's chest, under the head, over the shoulder to where the top starts, remembering to add seam allowance.

Materials

For a small dog

1½ ft. pink material

10 in. silver material

1½ ft. pink lining fabric

1 yd. pink mesh

1 yd. dark pink ribbon

A small piece of lightweight stiffener

A small piece of heavy-duty stiffener for the crown

1 yd. braid (to match your fabric)

A small piece of Velcro

Sequins or beads to decorate

1 Cut out all the dress pieces and iron on the lightweight stiffener to the wrong side of the center (silver) dress piece. Criss-cross and pin ribbon to center dress piece to look like lacing, and sew to the dress piece. Place the two side pieces of the dress to the center piece, right sides facing, pin, and machine stitch the pieces together with a small seam. Press the seam flat.

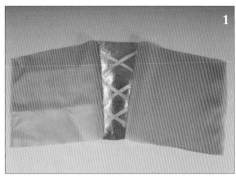

2 Place the lining over the dress top, right sides of material facing, pin, and stitch the sides and the top edge, leaving the bottom open to attach the skirt. Clip the corners and turn out to the right side. Press the seams flat. Turn under the lower, unstitched edges of the dress top and lining to wrong side by $1/3$ inch and press. Do not stitch yet.

3 Gather the three pieces of skirt net on the folded edges, to fit the waist edge between the dress and lining, leaving $1/2$ inch free at either end. Stitch all three gathered pieces together.

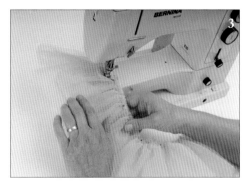

4 Place the gathered mesh pieces into the unstitched edge of the dress to fasten. Pin and stitch the dress, lining, and mesh together. Make the straps by folding the

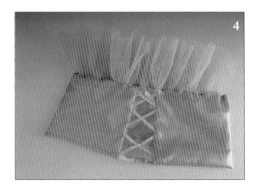

pieces in half lengthwise, right sides of material facing, pin, and stitch, leaving an opening of 6 inches at the center of each strap to take some gathered mesh. Mark the opening before you stitch this seam.

5 Place two pieces of the mesh shapes together and gather along the straight edge to fit into the unstitched opening of the strap. Fit the gathered mesh into the opening and hand stitch into place. Turn under the open end and stitch to neaten. Fit the straps onto the dress at the front, and tack. Try the dress on your dog and adjust the straps as necessary to ensure that the gathered mesh fits over your dog's shoulders.

6 Fasten the straps at the front of the dog by sewing Velcro onto the straps and the front of the dress. Stitch a piece of Velcro to the undersides of the dress to fasten under your dog's stomach. Decorate the dress and/or straps with little bows of ribbon, sequins, or flowers.

7 Cut out the crown shape in material and heavy duty stiffener. Iron the stiffener to the wrong side of one side of the material. Place the two pieces of crown together, right sides of material facing, pin and stitch the top

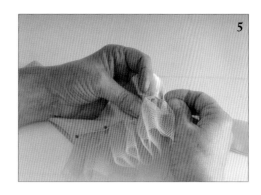

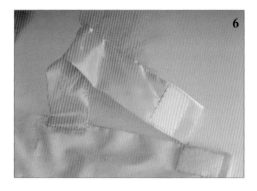

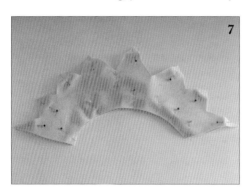

and bottom edges together. Clip all corners and curves close to the seam line and turn out to the right side. Press it well, ensuring that the points are eased out to the tips.

8 Turn the ends under and hand stitch together at the back to form the crown. Decorate with braid, sequins, rhinestones, or beads. Sew on a small piece of elastic to the sides of the crown to fit comfortably under your dog's chin.

SANTA CLAUS

What could be more fun than having a festive dog in the room, spreading yuletide cheer? This outfit is relatively simple to make and consists of a front piece, cloak, and hat. As with the other costumes made in this way, if you find your dog's legs slipping out of the leg tubes, you can easily tighten them at the top with a larger hem threaded with elastic. The Santa costume will, of course, look good on any dog, and if you make it well before Christmas, you could use photos of you and your pet in this fancy dress for your greeting cards. Scaled slightly larger, the hat will also fit humans, so you could make one for all the family. Our model is a young golden retriever named Tessa.

Materials

For a medium or large dog

1 yd. red material

1 yd. red lining

A small piece of black material for the belt and boots

A small piece of flesh-colored material for the hands

10 in. iron-on stiffener

1 yd. red ribbon

White wool for pom-pom

White fur or feather trimming

10 in. thin white elastic

Velcro for fastening

3 buttons and a small buckle

1 To make the hat, cut out two hat shapes in red felt or jacket fabric and two in iron on stiffener (heavyweight). Iron the stiffener to the hat shapes and place both pieces of the stiffened hat shapes together, right sides of material facing, pin, and stitch around the shape leaving the lower curve open, making a ¼-inch seam. Trim curves and turn hat right side out. Turn up the lower edge ¼ inch, pin, and stitch the hem down.

2 Make a white pom-pom (see Pierrot p. 17) and stitch to top of the hat. Decorate the lower edge of the hat with white fur trimming, swansdown, or, if these are not available, you could use white batting cut into strips. Stitch thin white elastic to each seam on the lower edge to fit your dog comfortably.

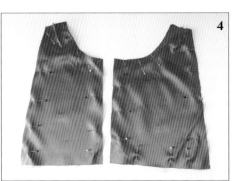

3 To make the front piece, cut out the jacket pieces and linings, sleeves and hand pieces, trousers, belt, and boot pieces, adjusting the length to fit your dog. Make a small dart on the wrong side of material at the shoulder edges of the jacket piece and the jacket lining. Press the darts flat.

4 Place the left piece of the lining to the left jacket piece, right sides of material facing, and pin around all edges. Sew lining to jacket ¼ inch from the edge, leaving an opening at the lower edge to turn out. Clip curves and trim corners, then turn out to the right side, easing out corners. Press it well. Repeat for the left side of jacket and stitch the openings together.

5 With right sides uppermost, pin the left side of the jacket over the right side and hand stitch down the front seam.

6 Make the belt by folding the material in half lengthwise, right side of material facing, pin, then stitch down one end and across the length, leaving one end open to turn out. Clip the corners. Turn out the belt to the right side, turn under open ends, and hand stitch together, then press it well. Put the buckle over the belt and place both on the jacket, then slip stitch into place.

7 Make the trousers and boots by placing one red leg piece to a black boot leg piece, right sides of material facing, and sew across. Repeat for the other leg. Press the seams open. Neaten both the top red edge and black edge with a small seam. Stitch together to form a tube, right sides of material facing, and turn out.

8 Sew to the top, positioning the leg parts on the wrong side of the jacket to fit your dog. Trim the lower edge of the jacket with white fur fabric or feather trim. Sew on three gold buttons to the front of the jacket.

9 Make the arms by placing a red top piece to a pink hand piece at the wrist edge, and sew together. Make up three other arm pieces in the same place. Place two pieces of arm and hand pieces together, right sides of material facing, then stitch around sleeve and hand, leaving a small opening to turn out. Clip curves.

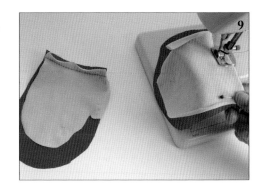

10 Turn each arm and hand to the right side and fill with batting, putting more stuffing into the arm than the hand. Sew up each opening, and machine stitch halfway up the hands to form fingers. Sew each arm to the appropriate sides of the jacket top. Finish by sewing red ribbon to each side of the neck edge to tie around your dog's neck.

11 Make the straps to fasten the cloak under the dog's stomach by placing

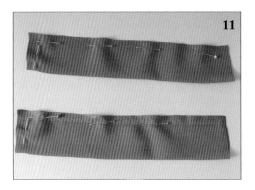

the strap pieces together, right sides of material facing. Pin, then stitch down one end and along the side, leaving an end open to turn out. Clip corners and turn it out to the right side. Press, and turn under the open end, then hand stitch into place. Sew Velcro onto both straps to fasten.

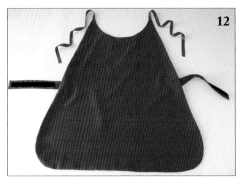

12 Place the cloak to the cloak lining, right sides of material facing. Pin, then stitch together, leaving a small opening on one side to turn out. Clip curves and corners and turn out to the right side. Press flat. Hand stitch the opening and sew a piece of ribbon to either side of the neck edge to fasten. Place the straps to each side of the cloak to suit your dog's waist, and stitch straps to the underside of the cloak.

54 Dress Up Your Dog

UNCLE SAM

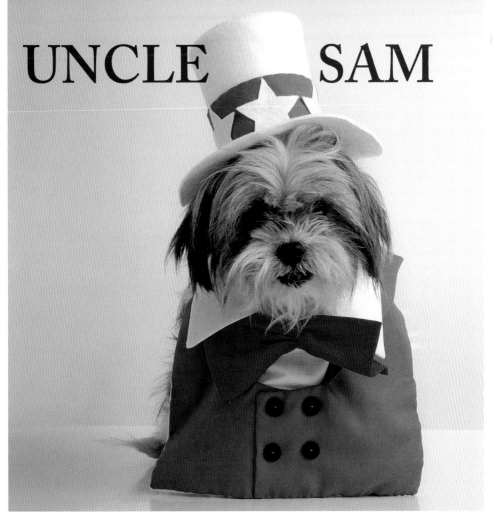

This little dog—Josh—was found starving and furless by the side of the road. Now nursed back to full health, he makes a superb Uncle Sam with his white beard. The outfit is a simple bib, which works well for smaller dogs, and is similar to the doll costumes made for Super Dog, Santa Claus, and Elvis, but without the arms and legs. Should your dog be taller, the pants and arms can be added (see instructions on the relevant pages). The arm sleeves would need to be blue, and the pants in red and white vertical stripes.

Materials

For a small dog

1½ ft. white material	10 in. heavy duty stiffening
10 in. blue material	1 yd. blue ribbon
Small piece red cotton or wide red ribbon for bow	4 black buttons
10 in. white felt	10 in. thin white elastic

1 Cut out all the top pieces and stiffening pieces, and place the two main white body pieces together, right sides of material facing, then sew around the outside edges, leaving the neck open to turn out. Clip corners and curves, and turn out to the right side. Press the seams.

2 Make the two collar pieces by folding each piece of fabric in half, right sides of material facing, and sew both ends. Clip the corners and turn out to the right side.

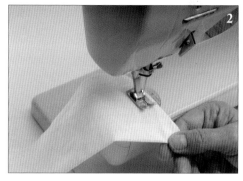

3 Place the collar pieces to each side of the body material, matching the back of the collar with the top seam and the front of the collar 1 inch from the center front of the body. They should be pinned on one side of the neck material, leaving the other piece free to neaten. Ease the collar over the

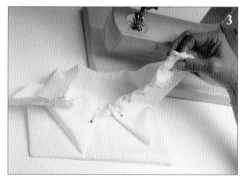

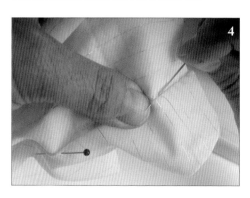

neckline so that it can follow the curve. Pin, tack, and stitch together. Clip curves, and press.

4 On the wrong side of the body piece, turn under the material at the neckline, and hand stitch over the seam line of the collar to neaten.

5 Make the jacket by placing each of the two pieces together, right sides of

material facing, pin, and sew around all outside edges, leaving openings on the lower edges to turn out. Clip curves and corners and turn each piece out to the right side, easing out all the corners. Press and sew up the openings.

6 Place the jacket pieces over the white top, matching the sides and lower edges, and overlapping the jacket fronts. Pin, and hand sew them together around the edges. Tack the jacket lapels to the white top on the top edge to prevent them from falling forward.

7 Sew on buttons, then pull collar to the front of jacket over the lapel, and press.

8 Make a bow by sewing a ¼-inch seam around the bow piece, right sides facing, and leaving an opening to turn it out. Trim corners, then turn out to right side and press, easing out the corners. Sew up the open edge. Mark the middle of the bow, and make a running stitch up the center point to gather it.

9 Stitch the bow to the white top, and finish the costume by sewing blue ribbon to each side of the neck edge to fasten around your dog's neck.

10 Cut out the hat pieces in white felt and heavy-duty iron-on stiffening. Iron the stiffening onto the brim, the middle, and the top. Place the two pieces of the brim together with the stiffening on the inside, and machine stitch all around the outside close to the edge.

11 Place the two pieces of the middle together, with the stiffening on the outside, and stitch together the top and bottom edges. Clip the curves and turn out to the right side. Press seams. Turn the two end pieces of the middle together, forming a tube, and hand stitch the two ends together.

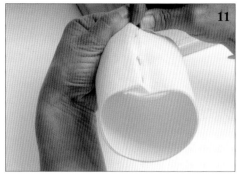

12 Stitch the tube to the brim on the lower edge, making sure that it is placed in the middle. Make the top piece in the same way that you made the brim, pin, and stitch the top to the tube with small over stitches.

13 Make the hat band by placing the two pieces of material together, right sides facing, then stitch down one end and the two long sides, clip curves and corners, and turn it out to the right side. Press, glue on some white stars cut from felt, then stitch to the hat. Finish the hat by stitching a thin piece of elastic on either side to fit under your dog's chin.

SUPER  DOG

Susie is a young and lively Fox terrier who was found abandoned by the side of a busy road. Having been nursed back to health, she has become extremely bouncy, to the point where it looks like she can fly, hence the Super Dog costume. The outfit consists of an all-in-one front piece and a cape. It is colorful, easy to make, and instantly recognizable. The sizes given are for a small dog, like Susie, so if your pet is larger, you will need to scale the costume by measuring your dog for height and leg length for the front piece, as well as the neck-to-tail length and width across your dog's back for the cape. Adjust all other measurements accordingly. As with many of the other costumes in this book, it will be quicker and easier to make if you leave out the lining, though it will not look so highly finished. As all dogs are different, you may need to tighten the top of the leg pieces with a larger hem threaded with elastic.

Materials

For a small dog

1½ ft. red material

1½ ft. red lining

10 in. blue material

10 in. blue lining

A small piece of yellow felt and a small piece of red felt for the belt and Super Dog emblem

A small piece of flesh-colored material for the hands

2½ ft. red ribbon

2½ ft. blue ribbon

Fabric glue

1. To make the front piece, cut out the top body piece, briefs, sleeves, hand pieces, legs, belt, and boot pieces in the appropriate colors, adjusting the lengths and widths to fit your dog. Make small darts on the wrong side of the material at each side of the shoulder edge of the top body piece. Press the darts flat.

2. Turn under the leg edges of the briefs. Press and pin the briefs to the right side of the body piece at the lower edge, matching the lower edge of the briefs to the lower edge of the body piece. Stitch the briefs to the body at the leg edges, and press flat.

3. Turn under the top and bottom edges of the belt, and press flat, then cut two small pieces of red ribbon to fit over the belt and pin them at equal distances from the center of the belt. Pin the belt to the body, just overlapping the top edge of the briefs, stitch on, and press flat.

4. Cut two circles in yellow felt just ¼ inch wider than the belt for the belt buckle, stack them together, and sew to the center of the belt. Make the Super Dog emblem by cutting out a piece of yellow felt to the shape indicated and a capital S and a capital D in red felt. Glue the letters onto the yellow background and allow them to dry for a few minutes. Stitch the letters onto the chest on the front of the top body piece.

5. Make a small dart on the wrong side of each shoulder edge on the lining material. Place the lining to the top body piece, wrong sides of material facing, and pin around all edges. Sew the lining to the top body piece ¼ inch from the edge, leaving an opening at the lower edge to turn it out to the right side.

Clip the curves and trim the corners, then turn it out to the right side, easing out the corners. Turn under the open, unstitched edges and hand stitch them together, then press flat. Stitch the blue ribbon to each shoulder edge to tie around your dog's neck.

6 Make the leg pieces with boots by turning under the top edges of each red boot piece and pinning it over the bottom edge of a blue leg piece on the right side of the material. Stitch them together. Repeat for the other leg. Press them flat.

7 Place the two long sides of the leg piece together, right sides of material facing, and stitch down the seam. Press the seam open. Neaten both the top blue edge and the red edge with a small hem, and stitch to the top on the wrong side of the jacket,

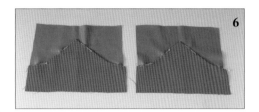

positioning the leg parts to fit your dog.

8 Make the arms by placing a blue top piece to a pink hand piece at the wrist edge, right sides of material facing, and sew together. Make the other three arm pieces in the same way.

9 Place two pieces of the arm and hand pieces together, right sides of material facing, and stitch around the sleeves and hands, leaving a small opening to turn out. Clip the curves and corners.

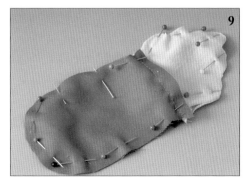

10 Turn the arm and hand out to the right side and fill with batting, putting more stuffing into the arm than the hand. Hand stitch the openings together and machine stitch halfway up the hand to form fingers, then sew an arm to each side of the body top. Sew ribbon on each side of the neck edge to tie.

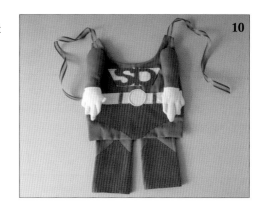

11 For the cape, make a Super Dog emblem in red and yellow felt as for the body, and stitch it to the center of the cape just below shoulder level. Place the cloak to the cloak lining, right sides of material facing. Pin, then stitch them together, leaving a small opening on one side to turn out. Clip the curves and corners, and turn out to the right side, sew the opening closed, and press flat. Sew ribbon to either side of neck edge to fasten.

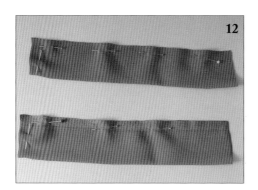

12 Make the straps to fasten under the dog's stomach by placing the strap pieces together, right sides of material facing. Pin, then stitch down one end and along the length, leaving an end open to turn out. Clip the corners and turn out to the right side, press, turn under the opening, and stitch closed.

13 Sew Velcro onto both straps, taking care that the Velcro with the hooks goes to the bottom piece of the strap so that it will not catch in the dog's fur as easily. Place the straps to each side of the cloak to fit your dog's waist, and stitch the straps to the underside of the cloak.

PIRATE

With the popularity of the pirate movies, this costume is topical and fun. It consists of a shirt, sash, and hat, and—if your dog is extremely calm and does not appear to mind wearing it—an eye patch makes a great accessory. As always, do not make your dog wear anything that causes discomfort. The shirt is made in cotton, as it is easy to use, will not make the dog hot, and, when finished with a bit of lace, looks dashing. The hat may look complicated, but is made in felt, which does not fray, and is actually quite easy to make. Use a brightly colored, silky material for the sash and inner hat to liven up the outfit. Our model, Archie, is a handsome sheltie who looks ready for some good swashbucklin'!

Materials

For a medium dog

2½ ft. white material for shirt

10 in. blue material for sash and hat

10 in. black felt

Black iron-on stiffening (very stiff)

2¾ yd. white lace, about 1 in. deep

1½ ft. gold braid

1½ ft. fringe (optional)

10 in. thin black elastic

5 ft. white elastic, ⅛–⅓ in. wide

5 ft. white bias binding ¾ in. wide

White Velcro

1 To make the hat, cut out all the hat pieces in felt and the iron-on stiffening. Iron the stiffening to the back, front, and base pieces of the hat, and stitch the gold braid onto the upper edges of the back and front pieces of the hat.

1

2 Neaten the blue, inner part of the hat with a small hem to avoid fraying. Make a pleat at each end of the inner hat material (see drawing) and stitch to each inner side of the hat pieces.

2

3

3 Pin the hat pieces together, and pin in the base part of the hat, ensuring that it is centered correctly.

4

4 Over stitch the hat together, starting 1 inch from the outer sides on the braided edge, then decorate the front of the hat with a skull and crossbones cut out of paper. Finish the hat by sewing on some thin black elastic to the base to fit comfortably under your dog's chin.

5 To make the sash, cut out the sash shape to fit around your dog's waist, tie up with a knot, and leave about 1½ feet to spare at each end. Neaten all edges with a small hem. If you wish to keep it simple, just leave as is, but if you feel adventurous, add some fringe and gold braid to each end.

6 Cut out the shirt piece and sleeves. Measure the position of the sleeve holes in the shirt very carefully, starting two-thirds of the way down from the folded edge, and the length from your dog's neck to shoulder plus 1¼ inches, then cut.

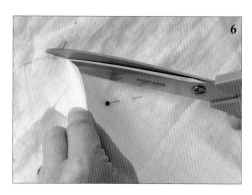

7 Turn up the bottom of the shirt sleeve edge by ¼ inch to the wrong side, and press down. Pin the lace over the turning and machine stitch the lace and hem. Do the same for the other sleeve.

8 Measure a line on each sleeve bottom, 1¼ inches from the lace edge, and pin the bias binding across the sleeve, then machine stitch the binding to the sleeve, close to the edge on each side of the binding, leaving the ends open to form a channel. Do the same for the other sleeve.

Dress Up Your Dog **65**

9 Cut two pieces of elastic to fit around your dog's front leg and, using a safety pin, thread the elastic through the channel of the binding. Secure the elastic at each side. Do the same for the other sleeve piece.

10 Gather both top edges of the sleeve to fit the armholes.

11 Pin sleeve sides together, and stitch a ¼-inch seam, then press it open.

12 As with the lower shirt sleeves, neaten lower edge of shirt by turning under ¼ inch of material to the wrong side, and press flat. Then pin lace to the turning on the wrong side, and machine stitch. Place bias binding across the shirt, 2 inches from the edge of the lower part of the shirt decorated with lace, then turn under each side of binding and stitch into place on both edges of binding, leaving sides open to make a channel to take elastic. Neaten underside edges of shirt by turning under a ½-inch hem and machine stitching into place.

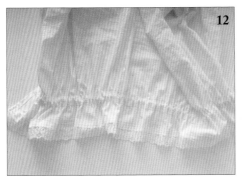

13 Turn ¼ inch of the material at the neck edge to the wrong side, and press. Turn under again by ½ inch, then press, pin, and machine stitch into place. Pin lace to the top edge of this seam on the wrong side and stitch very close to the top edge, leaving the sides open to take ribbon through the seam.

14 Position sleeves into the armholes, adjusting the gathers evenly, and pin into place, positioning the sleeve seam to the underarm edge of the sleeve hole so that it does not show when worn. Stitch the sleeves to the shirt piece, taking a ¼-inch seam.

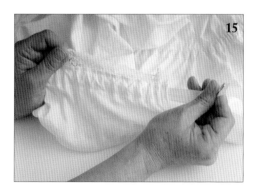

15 Thread ribbon through the neck channel to fit around your dog's neck comfortably, and stitch at both ends, leaving sufficient ribbon to tie a bow.

16 Sew Velcro onto each open edge of the shirt to fit your dog. Trim off any excess cotton ends from the shirt, and press.

CHEF

Not only does the chef costume suit Abi the basset, but she belongs to two retired chefs and is something of a gourmet herself. She certainly lives to eat. The jacket must, of course, be white and have two rows of buttons down the front. Most real chefs wear a blue or red cotton scarf to soak up perspiration and steam, and the traditional tall white hat is *de rigueur* in the kitchen. For fun, Abi has a wooden spoon attached to her costume, but its inclusion is recommended only if you're certain your dog won't chew it! The jacket here is lined, but it can be made without lining if you wish to create an easier version (be sure to neaten your seams if your fabric frays easily).

Materials

For a medium dog

1 yd. white cotton material

2½ ft. white lining

10 in. heavy-duty iron-on stiffener

10 in. blue or red cotton for the scarf

8 or 10 small white buttons

A small piece of white elastic to sew under hat

A small wooden spoon or other cooking implement
   (optional)

A piece of white ribbon or tape to hold spoon
   (optional)

1 To make the jacket, cut out all the jacket and lining pieces to fit your dog, then place the back and front pieces of the jacket together at underarm and shoulder edges, right sides of material facing. Pin, then stitch the side and underarm seams. Press the seams open, then repeat for the optional lining.

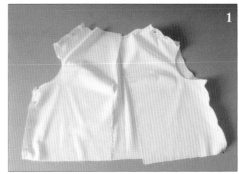

2 Make the collar by placing the back and side pieces of the collar together, right sides of material facing, then pin and stitch both side seams. Press both seams open. Repeat for the collar lining.

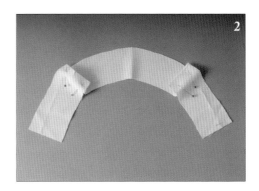

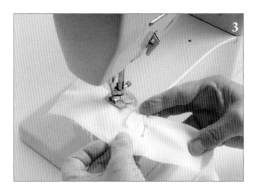

3 Place the collar and lining pieces together, right sides of material facing, then pin and stitch around the top (the inside curve) and side edges of the collar, taking a small seam. Clip the curves and corners, then turn out to the right side, and press flat.

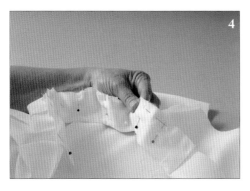

4 Place the collar to the neck edge of the jacket, matching the center back of the collar to the center back of the jacket and the shoulder seams. Tack the collar and jacket together.

5 With the right sides of material facing and seams matching, place the jacket lining over both the jacket and collar. Pin and stitch around all outside edges, leaving the sleeve holes open. Clip the curves and corners, then turn out to the right side. Pull out corners and edges, then press all the seams and the collar flat.

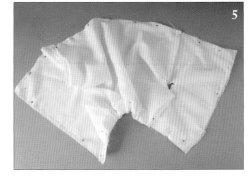

6 Join the underarm pieces of sleeve together, right sides of material facing, then pin and stitch them together. Press the seam open. Repeat for other sleeve and for both sleeve linings.

7 Place each sleeve and sleeve lining together, right sides of material facing, pin, and stitch the lower edges. Press the seam and turn it to the right side. Pin the sleeve and sleeve linings together at the top edge and gather stitch to ease the sleeve into the sleeve hole. (Use either a handmade running stitch or a large stitch on your machine.)

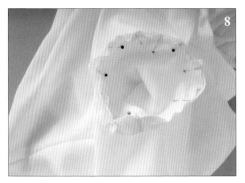

8 Fit the sleeve into the jacket (leaving the jacket lining free), with the sleeve seam at the bottom center of the sleeve hole. Pin or tack into place, then machine stitch all around the sleeve and jacket. Clip the curves and press around the seam.

9 Clip the curves of the unattached sleeve linings, turn under, and slipstitch over the sleeve seams to neaten.

10 Sew on Velcro to jacket fronts to fit your dog, then sew on the buttons to form two even rows down the front top edge of the jacket. If you want to, hand sew a small piece of ribbon onto one shoulder, making a slot to hold a small wooden spoon.

11 Cut out all the hat pieces and iron on the stiffening to the wrong side of the lower hat and hat lining. Place the hat and lining together, right sides of material facing, pin, and sew the lower edge. Press the seam open.

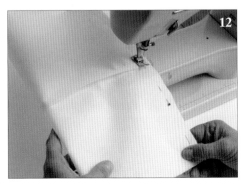

12 Put both of the side edges together, right sides of material facing, pin, and stitch the side seam. Press the seam open and turn the lining to the wrong side.

13 Pin the top edges of hat and lining together, and machine stitch.

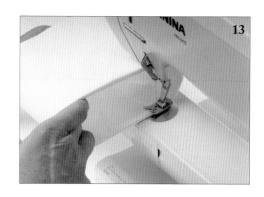

14 Pleat the top of the hat to fit the lower hat, and machine stitch the pleats into place.

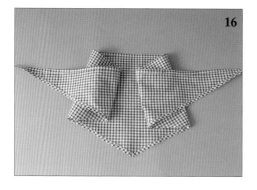

15 Turn under the pleated edge and pin to the top edge of the hat piece, then stitch the pleated top hat to the lower hat part. Finally, sew a piece of elastic to the bottom edge to fit under your dog's chin comfortably.

16 To make the scarf, cut out the scarf shape and hem all the edges. Cut off any hanging threads, and press well to finish.

ELVIS

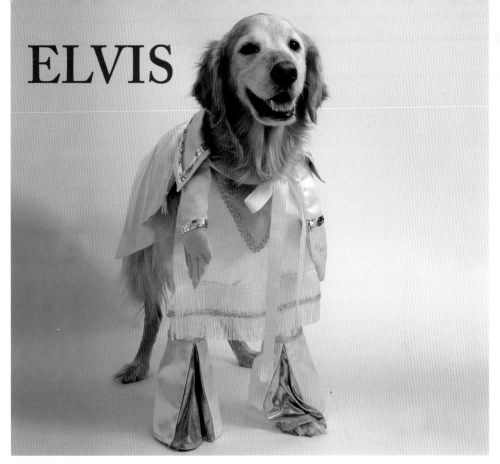

Buddy, a golden retriever, is owned by a singer who has a successful one-man show in Reno, so what could be more fitting for his costume? This outfit lets your imagination and creativity run wild. Spangles, sequins, and fringes were all used on Elvis's stage costumes, so yours can be as flashy as you like. The outfit is a little more complicated than some of the others that we have included, but I hope you will agree it is worth the effort. If you want to make a simpler version, you could leave the cape out. As with other, similar costumes, you may find that the leg pieces stay on better if you thread elastic through a channel at the top. Before you begin, measure your dog and make corresponding paper pattern pieces as in the diagrams.

Materials

For a medium or large dog

1 yd. white material

1 yd. white lining

Small piece of skin-colored fabric

1½ ft. silver material (or a contrast
    color of your choice)

2 yd. white ribbon

1 yd. silver braid

2 yd. white fringe

10 in. Velcro

10 in. iron-on stiffener (medium-weight)

Sequins or rhinestones to decorate (optional)

1 To make the front piece, cut out all pieces in material, lining, contrast material, and iron-on stiffening. Turn under a small hem on the skin-colored front piece, and pin it to the right side of the top front, then hand sew them together.

2 Trim the V-neck with braid on the right side, and make two small darts on each of the shoulder edges of the top and the top lining.

3 Place the lining to the top, right sides of material facing. Pin, then sew together, leaving a small opening to turn out. Turn out to the right side, press, and sew up the opening.

4 Trim the front of the top as you prefer. I have used fringe and silver braid.

5 To make the leg parts, join the center contrast piece to either side of the leg pieces. Press seams flat and repeat for the other leg. Fold into a pleat and pin the seams together. Stitch across the top to hold the pleat in place.

6 Pin the top piece of the leg part to the lower piece, right sides of material facing, and stitch together. Press the seams flat. If you wish to line the leg parts, then stitch a piece of lining to the top piece, right sides of material facing, and stitch together. Repeat for the other leg, then press all seams open.

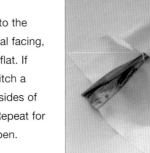

7 Stitch the back seam of the trouser bottom, top, and lining (if used) to form a tube. Repeat for the other leg.

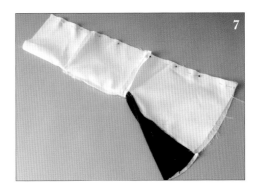

8 If you have used lining, turn under the lower edge, and stitch to the seam line to neaten. If not, just make a small hem at the edge of the leg part. Neaten the lower edge with a hem to fit your dog, and trim as you wish.

9 Sew leg parts to the back of the top to fit your dog, leaving the holes to put your dog's legs into.

10 Make the arms by placing a white top piece to a flesh-colored hand piece at the wrist edge, right sides of material facing, and sew together. Make the other three arm pieces in the same way. Put two of the arm and hand pieces together, right sides facing, and stitch around the sleeve and hand, leaving a small opening to turn out. Clip curves and turn out to the right side.

11 Fill each arm with batting, putting more stuffing into the sleeve than the hand, then sew up the opening and machine stitch halfway up the hand to make fingers. Sew an arm to both sides of the jacket top, then sew some ribbon to each shoulder to tie around your dog's neck.

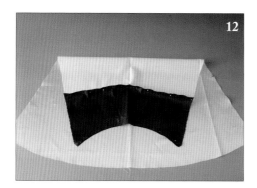

12 To make the cape, cut out all cape pieces in white fabric, contrast fabric, and stiffener. Iron the stiffener to the wrong side of the top contrast piece, then pin the contrast piece to the main part of the cape as shown. Stitch together, clip a small V at the center of the new seam, and press. Stitch the two lining pieces (if you choose to line your cape) using the same method.

13 Make the collar by ironing the stiffener to the wrong side of the contrast piece of collar, place the white collar piece and the stiffened contrast piece together, right sides of material facing, pin, and stitch sides and long edge, leaving the neck edge unstitched.

14 Clip corners and curves, turn to right side, and press well.

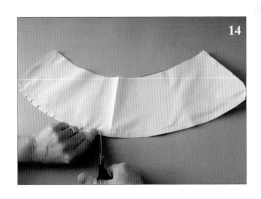

15 Tack collar together at the neck edge that was left open, and pin this edge to the neck edge of the cape, making sure that the collar is placed ½ inch from the side edges. Tack together.

16 Place the lining over the cape and collar, right sides of material facing, pin, and stitch all around the cape and neck edge, leaving a small opening at the lower edge of the cape to pull through and make sure that the collar inside is not caught in the stitching. Clip curves and corners, turn out to right side, press well, and stitch the opening together.

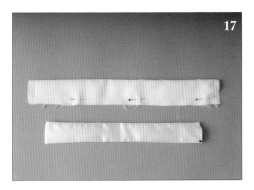

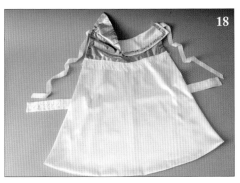

17 Make two straps (as for Santa Claus and Super Dog) using white material, and attach them to the lining side of the cape to fit around your dog's chest comfortably. Sew on Velcro to the ends.

18 Decorate your cape and collar as desired, and sew ribbon onto each side of the neck edge to fasten around your dog's neck.

PATTERNS

Rapper
page 12

Rapper pattern pieces:

Behind the neck
to three-quarters of your
dog's back
plus 1-inch seam

Fold

Top body part
Cut one on fold

Middle of dog's back
to top of leg plus ¹/₂ inch

Under body part
Cut two

Width of the widest
part of your dog's leg
plus 1-inch seams

It is advisable to make the pattern peices in paper
using your dog's measurements before you cut your fabric.
*Don't forget to add seam allowance of ¹/₂-inch per seam.

Pierrot Costume

page 15

Pierrot pattern pieces:

*These sizes are for a large dog, so you will need to scale them down for a smaller dog.

Black material, 5 feet x 8 inches

White material, 5 feet x 6½ inches

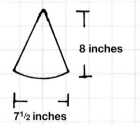

8 inches

7½ inches

Cut one in white felt
Cut one in black felt
Cut two in stiffening

Frenchman

page 18

Frenchman pattern pieces:

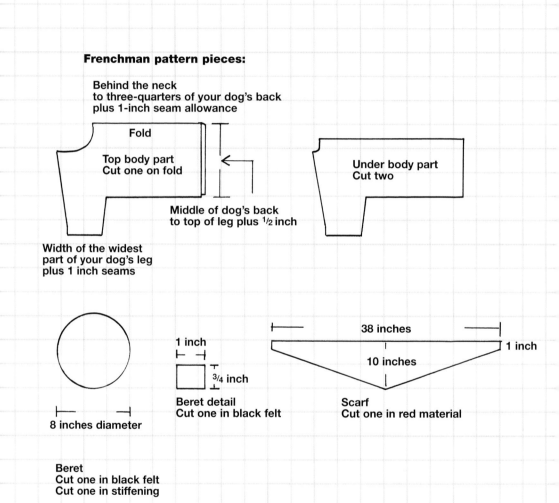

Behind the neck
to three-quarters of your dog's back
plus 1-inch seam allowance

Fold

Top body part
Cut one on fold

Under body part
Cut two

Middle of dog's back
to top of leg plus ½ inch

Width of the widest
part of your dog's leg
plus 1 inch seams

8 inches diameter

1 inch

¾ inch

Beret detail
Cut one in black felt

38 inches

1 inch

10 inches

Scarf
Cut one in red material

Beret
Cut one in black felt
Cut one in stiffening

These measurements are for a small dog, so
you will need to adjust them for your pet.

Hippy

page 21

Hippy pattern pieces:

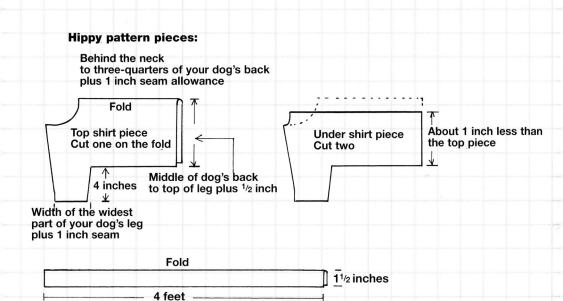

Behind the neck
to three-quarters of your dog's back
plus 1 inch seam allowance

Fold

Top shirt piece
Cut one on the fold

4 inches

Middle of dog's back
to top of leg plus ½ inch

Width of the widest
part of your dog's leg
plus 1 inch seam

Under shirt piece
Cut two

About 1 inch less than
the top piece

Fold

1½ inches

4 feet

Headband
Cut one on the fold

Witch

page 24

Witch pattern pieces:

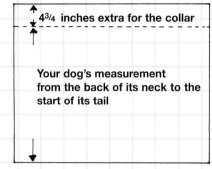

4³/4 inches extra for the collar

Your dog's measurement
from the back of its neck to the
start of its tail

The length of your dog over its
back paw to paw

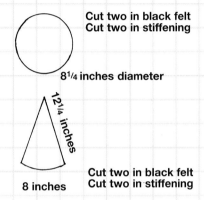

Cut two in black felt
Cut two in stiffening

8¹/4 inches diameter

12¹/4 inches

8 inches

Cut two in black felt
Cut two in stiffening

Flower

page 28

Flower pattern pieces:

The measurement of your dog's neck plus 1½ inches
Cut one

3 inches

Large white petal
Cut seven

6 inches

4¼ inches

Medium yellow petal
Cut six

4³/4 inches

3½ inches

Small white petal for hat
Cut six

3½ inches

2¼ inches

2¼ inches diameter
Cut two in yellow

Leaf hat shape
Cut two in green

5½ inches

7 inches

Make a paper template for the petals
and leaf before you cut the fabric.
Fold a peice of paper in half and cut
as in diagram.

Angel

page 31

Angel pattern pieces:

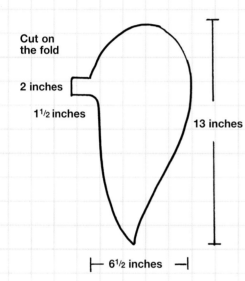

Cut on
the fold

2 inches

1½ inches

13 inches

6½ inches

Angel wings: cut on the fold
Cut two in white felt
Cut one in stiffening
Cut one in batting

*These sizes are for a small dog, so
you will need to adjust them for a
larger dog.

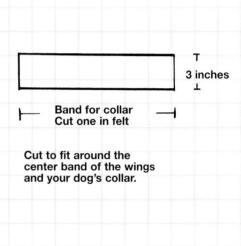

3 inches

Band for collar
Cut one in felt

Cut to fit around the
center band of the wings
and your dog's collar.

Devil

page 34

Devil pattern pieces:

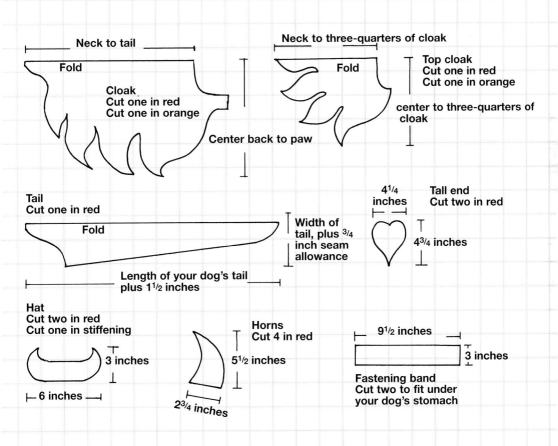

Neck to tail

Fold

Cloak
Cut one in red
Cut one in orange

Center back to paw

Neck to three-quarters of cloak

Fold

Top cloak
Cut one in red
Cut one in orange

center to three-quarters of cloak

Tail
Cut one in red

Fold

Width of tail, plus $3/4$ inch seam allowance

Length of your dog's tail plus $1 1/2$ inches

$4 1/4$ inches

Tall end
Cut two in red

$4 3/4$ inches

Hat
Cut two in red
Cut one in stiffening

3 inches

6 inches

Horns
Cut 4 in red

$5 1/2$ inches

$2 3/4$ inches

$9 1/2$ inches

3 inches

Fastening band
Cut two to fit under your dog's stomach

Monk

page 38

Monk pattern pieces:

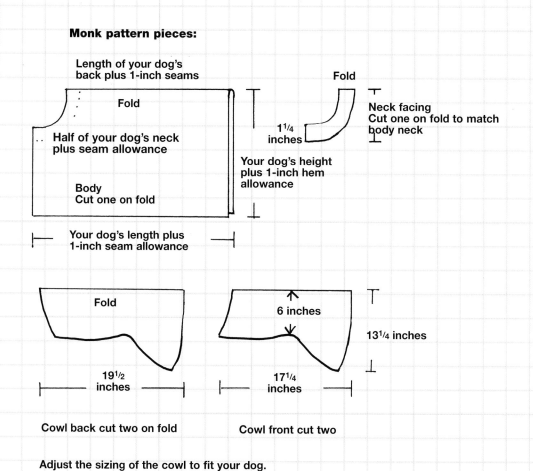

Length of your dog's
back plus 1-inch seams

Fold

Fold

Neck facing
Cut one on fold to match
body neck

Half of your dog's neck
plus seam allowance

1¼
inches

Your dog's height
plus 1-inch hem
allowance

Body
Cut one on fold

Your dog's length plus
1-inch seam allowance

Fold

6 inches

13¼ inches

19½
inches

17¼
inches

Cowl back cut two on fold

Cowl front cut two

Adjust the sizing of the cowl to fit your dog.

Hawaiian Girl

page 41

Hawaiian Girl pattern pieces:

$3^1/_2$
inches

Waist band
Cut one in material
Cut one in stiffening

The width around your dog's
stomach plus $2^1/_4$ inches

$10^1/_2$
inches

Bikini top
Cut one in material

The width around your dog's chest
plus 1 foot.

$3^1/_2$ inches

$3^1/_2$
inches

Lei flower
Cut about fifty

Cleopatra

page 44

Cleopatra pattern pieces:

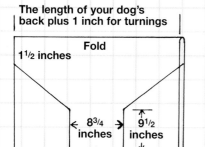

The length of your dog's
back plus 1 inch for turnings

Fold

1½ inches

8¾
inches

9½
inches

Center under dog's stomach

3 inches

The measurement around your
dog's neck plus 1 inch.

7 inches

Coat
Cut two in material
Cut one in interlining

Collar
Cut two in gold
Cut two in stiffening

Princess

page 48

Princess pattern pieces:

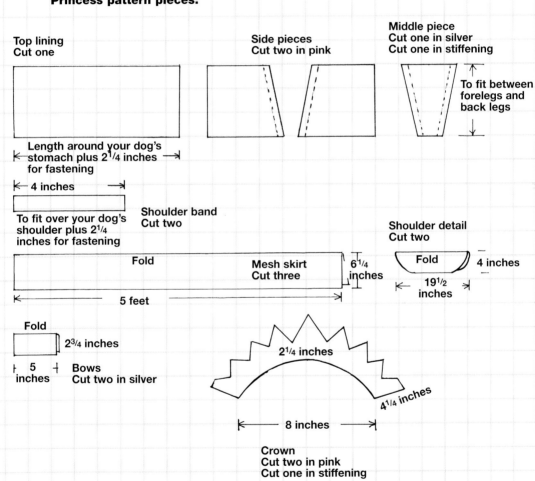

Top lining
Cut one

Length around your dog's
stomach plus 2¼ inches
for fastening

4 inches

To fit over your dog's
shoulder plus 2¼
inches for fastening

Side pieces
Cut two in pink

Middle piece
Cut one in silver
Cut one in stiffening

To fit between
forelegs and
back legs

Shoulder band
Cut two

Fold

Mesh skirt
Cut three

6¼
inches

5 feet

Shoulder detail
Cut two

Fold

4 inches

19½
inches

Fold

2¾ inches

5
inches

Bows
Cut two in silver

2¼ inches

4¼ inches

8 inches

Crown
Cut two in pink
Cut one in stiffening

Santa Claus

page 51

Santa Claus pattern pieces:

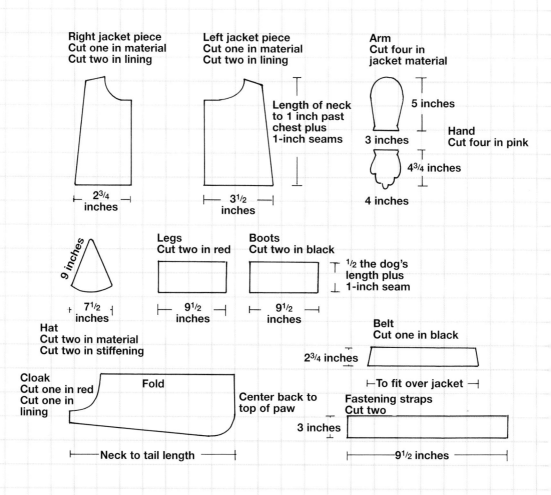

Right jacket piece
Cut one in material
Cut two in lining

2³/₄ inches

Left jacket piece
Cut one in material
Cut two in lining

Length of neck
to 1 inch past
chest plus
1-inch seams

3¹/₂ inches

Arm
Cut four in
jacket material

5 inches

3 inches

Hand
Cut four in pink

4³/₄ inches

4 inches

9 inches

7¹/₂ inches

Hat
Cut two in material
Cut two in stiffening

Legs
Cut two in red

9¹/₂ inches

Boots
Cut two in black

9¹/₂ inches

¹/₂ the dog's
length plus
1-inch seam

Belt
Cut one in black

2³/₄ inches

To fit over jacket

Cloak
Cut one in red
Cut one in
lining

Fold

Center back to
top of paw

3 inches

Fastening straps
Cut two

Neck to tail length

9¹/₂ inches

Uncle Sam

page 55

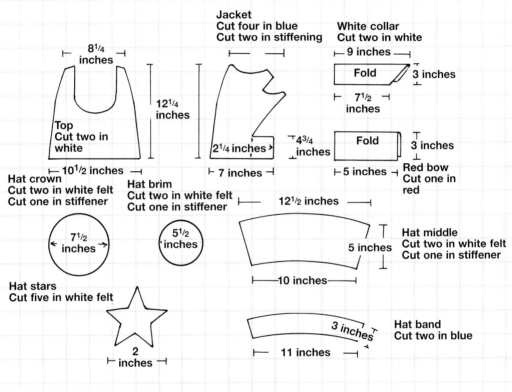

Uncle Sam pattern pieces:

Jacket
Cut four in blue
Cut two in stiffening

White collar
Cut two in white

├─ 9 inches ─┤

Fold · 3 inches

├─ 7½ inches ─┤

8¼ inches

12¼ inches

Top
Cut two in white

├─10½ inches ─┤

2¼ inches

4¾ inches

├─ 7 inches ─┤

Fold · 3 inches

├─5 inches ─┤

Red bow
Cut one in red

Hat crown
Cut two in white felt
Cut one in stiffener

7½ inches

Hat brim
Cut two in white felt
Cut one in stiffener

5½ inches

├─ 12½ inches ─┤

5 inches

Hat middle
Cut two in white felt
Cut one in stiffener

├──10 inches──┤

Hat stars
Cut five in white felt

2 inches

3 inches

├─ 11 inches ─┤

Hat band
Cut two in blue

*These sizes are for a small dog, so you will need to adjust them for your pet.

Super Dog
page 59

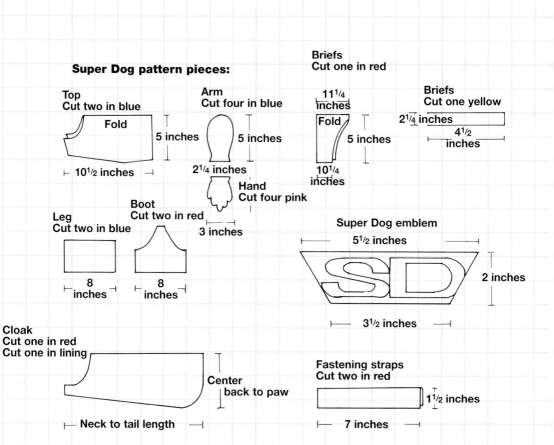

Super Dog pattern pieces:

Top
Cut two in blue

Fold

5 inches

⊢ 10½ inches ⊣

Arm
Cut four in blue

5 inches

2¼ inches

Hand
Cut four pink

Briefs
Cut one in red

11¼ inches

Fold

5 inches

10¼ inches

Briefs
Cut one yellow

2¼ inches

4½ inches

Leg
Cut two in blue

8 inches

Boot
Cut two in red

3 inches

8 inches

Super Dog emblem

5½ inches

2 inches

3½ inches

Cloak
Cut one in red
Cut one in lining

Center
back to paw

⊢ Neck to tail length ⊣

Fastening straps
Cut two in red

1½ inches

⊢ 7 inches ⊣

*These sizes are for a small
dog, so you will need to adjust
them for your pet.

Pirate

page 63

Pirate pattern pieces:

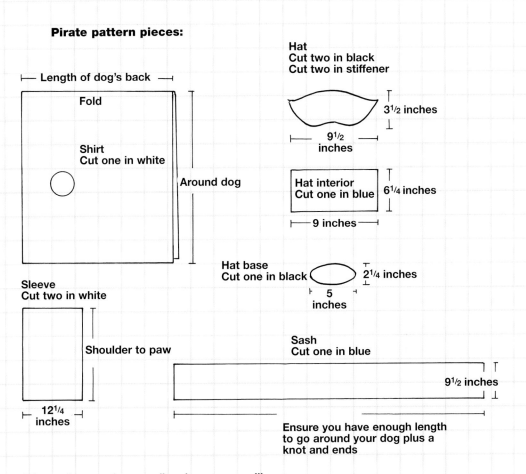

├─ Length of dog's back ─┤

Fold

Shirt
Cut one in white

Around dog

Hat
Cut two in black
Cut two in stiffener

3½ inches

├─── 9½ ───┤
inches

Hat interior
Cut one in blue 6¼ inches

├──── 9 inches ────┤

Hat base
Cut one in black 2¼ inches

├─ 5 ─┤
inches

Sleeve
Cut two in white

Shoulder to paw

├─ 12¼ ─┤
inches

Sash
Cut one in blue

9½ inches

Ensure you have enough length
to go around your dog plus a
knot and ends

*These sizes are for a mediun dog, so you will
need to adjust them for your pet.

Chef

page 68

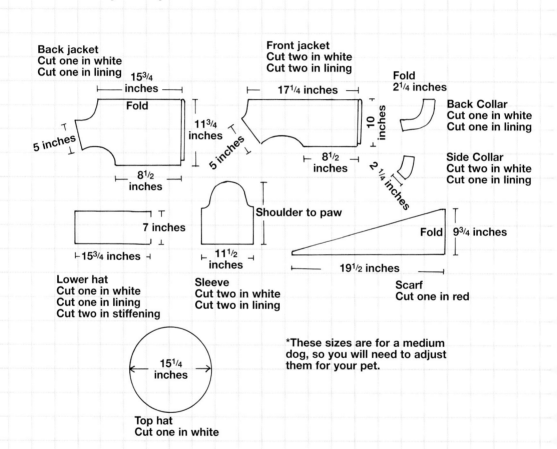

Chef pattern pieces:

Back jacket
Cut one in white
Cut one in lining

15¾ inches
Fold
5 inches
11¾ inches
8½ inches

Front jacket
Cut two in white
Cut two in lining

17¼ inches
5 inches
10 inches
8½ inches

Fold
2¼ inches

Back Collar
Cut one in white
Cut one in lining

Side Collar
Cut two in white
Cut one in lining

2¼ inches

7 inches
15¾ inches

Lower hat
Cut one in white
Cut one in lining
Cut two in stiffening

Shoulder to paw

11½ inches

Sleeve
Cut two in white
Cut two in lining

Fold 9¾ inches

19½ inches

Scarf
Cut one in red

*These sizes are for a medium
dog, so you will need to adjust
them for your pet.

15¼ inches

Top hat
Cut one in white

Elvis

page 73

Elvis pattern pieces:

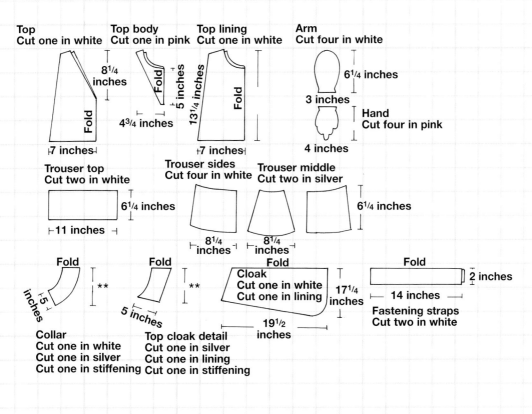

Top
Cut one in white

8¼ inches

Fold

┤7 inches├

Top body
Cut one in pink

Fold

5 inches

4¾ inches

Top lining
Cut one in white

13¼ inches

Fold

┤7 inches├

Arm
Cut four in white

6¼ inches

3 inches

Hand
Cut four in pink

4 inches

Trouser top
Cut two in white

6¼ inches

├11 inches ┤

Trouser sides
Cut four in white

8¼ inches

Trouser middle
Cut two in silver

8¼ inches

6¼ inches

Fold

5 inches

**

Collar
Cut one in white
Cut one in silver
Cut one in stiffening

Fold

5 inches

**

Top cloak detail
Cut one in silver
Cut one in lining
Cut one in stiffening

Fold

Cloak
Cut one in white
Cut one in lining

17¼ inches

19½ inches

Fold

2 inches

├ 14 inches ┤

Fastening straps
Cut two in white

** Same size as neck edge of top
cloak

* These sizes are for a large dog,
so you will need to adjust them
for your pet.

Handy Hints

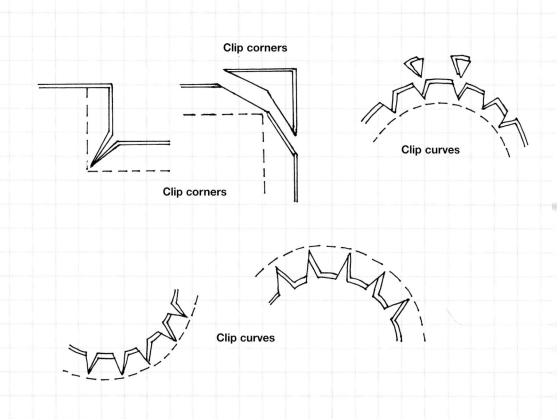

Clip corners

Clip corners

Clip curves

Clip curves